DOODLE SOUP

Poems by

JOHN CIARDI

Illustrated by Merle Nacht

HOUGHTON MIFFLIN COMPANY   BOSTON   1985

Library of Congress Cataloging in Publication Data

Ciardi, John
   Doodle soup.

   Summary: Thirty-eight poems, mostly humorous,
by the well-known poet.
   1. Children's poetry, American. [1. American poetry. 2. Humorous poetry] I. Title.
PS3505.I27D6   1985   811'.52   85-814
ISBN 0-395-38395-1

Printed in the United States of America

V 10 9 8 7 6 5 4 3 2 1

for Mrs. Graves B. Erskine,
    our beloved Aunt Connie,
    because she likes poems,
    and because she is the great lady
    the nicest little girl in town grows up to be.

CONTENTS

The Old Lady in Bumbletown	3
The Dangers of Taking Baths	4
The Dollar Dog	5
About Trapping in the North Woods	6
About Indians	8
Pennies from Heaven	10
At Night	11
There's Nothing to It	12
All I Did Was Ask My Sister a Question	13
The Best Part of Going Away Is Going Away from You	14
"I Am Home," Said the Turtle	15
I Know I'm Sweet, But!	16
How I Helped the Traveler	17
The Chap Who Disappeared	18
Why Pigs Cannot Write Poems	20
The Baseball Player	22
It Makes No Difference to Me	23
Doing a Good Deed	24
Do You Feel Sorry for Him?	26
How Time Goes	27
How Much Is a Gross?	28
I Picked a Dream Out of My Head	29
In Pete's Shoes	30
I Don't Think It Would Pay to Give You a Job	32
I Made Him Welcome but He Didn't Stay	34
Ding-a-Ling	36
Sometimes It Pays to Back Up	38

Frizzing   39
At the Beach   40
It Really Wasn't Too Bad   42
A Lesson in Manners   44
About Being Very Good etc.   46
The Glass Canoe   48
There Was a Man from Nowhere   50
The Old Salt   52
Now About Tigers   54
Sometimes There Is No Easy Answer   56
Good-bye   57

DOODLE SOUP

The Old Lady in Bumbletown

There was an old lady in Bumbletown.
She had three black cats and five were brown.
She had two red cows and three were blue.
Which is rather strange, but so are you.

The Dangers of Taking Baths

Jimmy Jones was skin and bones.
    The bone was mostly in his head.
He used the skin to take baths in,
    But he caught cold and now he's dead.

Don't be a bonehead. Heaven knows
    Soap is not good for the eyes.
And suds leak in right through the skin.
    Adam, in man's first Paradise,

Had no tub nor need to scrub.
    And he was no bonehead.
By saying "Nope" to water and soap
    He lived till he was dead.

The Dollar Dog

I had a dollar dog named Spot.
He wasn't much, but he was a lot
Of *kinds* of dog, plus a few parts flea,
Seven parts yapper, and seventy-three
Or seventy-four parts this-and-that.
The only thing he wasn't was cat.
He was collie-terrier-spaniel-hound
And everything else they have at the pound.
Yes, some might call him a mongrel, but
To me he was thoroughbred, pedigreed mutt.
A middle-sized nothing, or slightly smaller,
But a lot of kinds to get for a dollar.

About Trapping in the North Woods

The trouble with catching a bull moose
      Is that it's mean. And also large.
Try to hold fast. If you let loose,
      The moose may lower its head and charge.

If you hold on, you won't be there.
      Not when it starts to toss its head
With you on the antlers. You'll be in the air
      And trying to hope you are not dead.

If you do let go, its charge is a bit
      Like seven freight trains side by side
On a single track. What you see of it
      Is *too* near, *too* fast, and *too* wide.

Moose tend to have a mind of their own.
      Don't try to change it — they may be right.
My advice to you is LEAVE THEM ALONE
      (Unless you are braver than you are bright).

About Indians

When Indians are sleepy
They go into a teepee
And close the flap
And take a nap
And dream of antelope and deer
Until a squaw says, "Now see here!
You going to sleep all night and day?
Get up and shoot a bear, I say!
We need the hide. We need the meat.
We need the grease. — Up on your feet!"

Then Indians get up and grunt
And go off in the woods and hunt
And shoot a bear and drag it in
And leave it for the squaws to skin.

At which point, feeling sleepy
They creep back to the teepee
And close the flap
And take a nap.

Then all there is
Is *zzzz...zzzz...zzzz.*
Try some. That's right.
Heap fine! ...g o o d   n i g h t...

Pennies from Heaven

There once was a jack on a steeple.
 He was painting it copper brown.
He dribbled paint on the people
 On the sidewalk eight flights down.

They thought it was raining pennies.
 They ran for their piggy banks.
And whenever they caught a drop in the slot
 They shouted, "Many thanks!"

Whenever they caught a drop in the slot
 They dreamed of what they would buy.
But they cried a lot, for they often got
 A drop or two in the eye.

They cried even more when they went to the store
 With their money and tried to spend it.
But it helps to cry when there's paint in your eye.
 And the steeple does look splendid!

At Night

When I am outdoors and begin
To start to think about going in,
I wait a minute, then five, then ten,
Then start to begin to wait again
Before I start to begin to go.
Now you may think it is much too slow
To wait so long to start to begin
To think about starting to go in.
But once it starts to begin to get late,
In half a flash it is half-past eight,
And time to wash and say good night,
And get into bed and douse the light,
And twist the covers into a heap.
And then, all at once — you've gone to sleep!

There's Nothing to It

What's half of nothing? I have no pie.
Now suppose I cut it in two and I
Give you a piece. Then your sister Sue
Says, "Please, may I have some no-pie, too?"
So I cut my piece in two again
And give Sue half of that. Now — when
I gave you half, it was half of all
The nothing I had. Sue, you recall,
Got half of my half. — Who got less?
If you're not sure, would you care to guess?
Sue did? Oh, come now, Sue. Don't cry.
Here's my piece. There. Enjoy your pie!

All I Did Was Ask My Sister a Question

Why is water wet?   Let's see —
Because...   Well, silly, it has to be!
How could you drink it if it were dry?
If you got a drop of it in your eye
It would sting like sand and make you cry.
When it started to rain, it would come down dust.
You'd have to hold your breath till you bust
Or turn to powder inside your chest.
And how would I pass my swimming test
And get my badge?   Not that you'd care.
You'd still be standing around somewhere
Asking foolish questions to get me mad!
Well, I'll tell Mother and she'll tell Dad.
Then see what he does to you for that!
And see if I care, you little brat!

The Best Part of Going Away
Is Going Away from You

If I could borrow a rocket ship,
I'd pack a bag and take a trip
To the other side of twice as far
From nowhere near wherever you are.
And if there wasn't time to pack,
I'd just blast off, and never come back!

"I Am Home," Said the Turtle

"I am home," said the turtle, as it pulled in its head
And its feet, and its tail. "I am home, and in bed.

"No matter what inches and inches I roam,
When the long day is done, I am always at home.

"I may go whole feet…even yards…in a day,
But I never get lost, for I'm never away

"From my snug little house and my snug little bed.
Try being a turtle! — That's using your head!

"You can go on forever, no matter how far,
And whatever you need is wherever you are!"

("Is there one thing I miss when I'm snuggled in tight?
Yes: there's no room for someone to kiss me good night.")

I Know I'm Sweet, But!

A cross-eyed bee went looking for honey.
It sniffed a rose, then it sniffed me.
And OUCH! — I tell you it's not funny
To be taken for a rose by a cross-eyed bee!

How I Helped the Traveler

Main Street? Yessir. Let me see —
If it isn't this street, it must be
The next or the next on the left or right.
Just go down here to the traffic light
And take a turn, or go straight ahead.
(You have to stop if the light is red.)
— That could be Main. If it's not Main,
Go round the block and try again.
You just can't miss it. It's in plain sight:
Straight ahead, or left, or right.

The Chap Who Disappeared

There was a drowsy sort of chap
Who went upstairs to take a nap.

At least that's where he thought he went.
But he was living in a tent.

It's true he hadn't pitched it yet,
Which may have caused him to forget

He hadn't brought a single stair
To climb up to what wasn't there.

Or it may be he never knew
Two-story tents are very few.

So few that there are none at all.
Which left him in the upper hall

Of nowhere. Which may well explain
Why he was never seen again.

Why Pigs Cannot Write Poems

Pigs cannot write poems because
Nothing rhymes with *oink*. If you
Think you can find a rhyme, I'll pause,
But if I wait until you do,
I'll have forgotten why it was
Pigs cannot write poems because.

The Baseball Player

— What's the score?
— Two hundred to four.
— It looks like the other team's day.
— Well, you can bet
   We're not through yet:
   We still have an inning to play!

It Makes No Difference to Me

I climbed a mountain three feet high
And banged my head against the sky.

"Watch out!" my sister's brother said.
"You climb that high, you'll lose your head!"

I didn't care. Mine is no use
To anyone. What's your excuse?

Doing a Good Deed

At the foot of the hill, the ice cream truck
Drove into a mudhole and got stuck.
We helped the driver back on the road.
But first we had to lighten the load.
When we had helped a gallon apiece,
The driver phoned the Chief of Police,
Who drove a pole into the sludge
And measured five feet of chocolate fudge
That had to be lightened. Well, we turned to
And helped the man. What else could we do?
I even called my Boy Scout Troop.
By then there was nothing left but soup.
Still, ice cream soup is very good.
And we wanted to help as much as we could.
It was our good deed for the day
To help the man get on his way.
At last we pulled him out of the muck,
And he drove away in his empty truck,
Thanking us all for helping him out.
That made us happy. For there's no doubt
We must help our neighbor as much as we can.
Especially when he's the ice cream man.

Do You Feel Sorry for Him?

Have you heard what happened to Ricky Rose?
    He climbed a tree to rob a nest
And the mother bird pecked off his nose.
    If he ever stops crying I'll tell you the rest.
(I can tell you now, in so many words:
Robbing nests is for the birds!)

How Time Goes

How old am I? I really don't know,
　　But I can tell you I have spent
My whole life — up to a minute ago —
　　Being younger than I am now. I meant
To keep it that way, I suppose,
But that's how it is with time — it goes.

How Much Is a Gross?

Here come a dozen kangaroos
Wearing a gross of tennis shoes.
How many is a gross? Don't guess.
A gross is not a more-or-less.
It is precisely an amount.
If you don't know, I'll help you count.

To start with, you must realize
Few kangaroos can find their size
In tennis shoes. They have to put
Six of the things on either foot
To get one big enough. They rip them
Front and back, and then they slip them,
Six on the left, six on the right,
Then get some string and tie them tight.
Then slap the ground and off they thump,
Six shoes to a thumper, twelve to a jump.
Multiply by twelve kangaroos
And that's a gross of tennis shoes.

I Picked a Dream Out of My Head

I picked a dream out of my head
When I was fast asleep.
It was about a fish that said,
"I am too small to keep!"

I threw it back and tried again.
That time I dreamed a yak
That said to me, "It looks like rain:
I'd best be starting back!"

I picked another one about
A tiger in a top hat.
It snarled so that I had to shout,
"This is my dream: you stop that!"

There was one more though I forgot
Just what it was and said,
But all the same that is a lot
To find in just one head.

In Pete's Shoes

I tried to tell my small son Pete
He had his shoes on the wrong feet.

That's when he explained to his silly Dad
Those were the only feet he had —

How could they be wrong? I had to agree
He made some sense, for I could see

He had one shoe here and one shoe there,
And neither one of his feet was bare.

What's wrong with that? I racked my brain
Trying to think of a way to explain.

I thought till my head began to ache.
I was sure there had been some mistake.

For I could see as we walked along
That his left was right and his right was wrong.

But just as sure as I'm his dad
Those *were* the only feet he had.

The answer came to me late that night:
Cross out what's wrong and what's left is right.

What I had left was my small son Pete
Who knows how to stand on his own two feet.

Though if I'm given a chance to choose,
I'd rather not be in his shoes.

I Don't Think It Would Pay
to Give You a Job

I use a sheep to cut my grass.
    It is easy to start and it seldom stops.
It needs no oiling. It uses no gas.
    And in winter it turns into mutton chops.

I use three geese to weed my garden.
    I like their work. What I like most,
When they are through, is how well they do
    As a fragrant Christmas roast.

I guess I could pay you a penny or three
    If you worked from sun to sun.
What I can't see is what good you'd be
    When all the work has been done.

I Made Him Welcome but
He Didn't Stay

I'm glad you came! My crocodile
    Is always happy when you come by.
Just look at him wag his tail and smile!
    Just look at the eager gleam in his eye!

He wants to play! You needn't fear:
    I fed him less than a month ago.
Yes, he's a pig! Now that you're here
    He will beg for food. You must tell him *No!*

When you come, all my pets begin
    To dance around. My grizzly bear
Wants you to see how wide he can grin.
    My wolf keeps leaping into the air

As if he wanted to break his chain
    And jump on your back and lick your ear.
My tiger starts screaming as if in pain,
    But he only means he's glad you're here.

Do please come in. Would you like a swim?
     My shark likes company in the pool.
It does get rather lonely for him
     Now that the fish are away in school.

After you splash around for a while,
     I hope you will join us. I have a hunch
My bear will say to my crocodile,
     "Let's ask if we can have him for lunch!"

— Where is that boy? I turned my head
     To scold my pets for carrying on
Too playfully. "Behave!" I said.
     And when I turned back — he was gone!

Ding-a-Ling

Is that you, Willy? Well, hello.
I thought I'd call to let you know
Someone just called to ask about you.
I had to tell him it was true.
He said, "Hm, yes. Just as I thought!"
Yes, he told me his name, but I forgot.
I have to tell you his voice was rough!
It sounded as deep and mean and tough
As if he had gravel in his craw
And was chewing the teeth from a rusty saw.
— Can you guess who? I have a hunch
It was probably Deputy Sheriff Crunch.
As he hung up I heard him say,
"I am going to get him, and this is the day!"
No, I'm not *sure* that's what he said.
I started to ask but the line went dead.

If he's after you, you had better hide.
First go to the window and look outside:
If a squad car's there with a flashing light
I will have to guess I have guessed right,
And he's coming to get you for skipping school.
I'll wait. — What? Nothing? — APRIL FOOL!

Sometimes It Pays to Back Up

It doesn't do to push too hard
    Against an elephant or a mule
When it's pushing back. If it gains a yard
    You lose one as a general rule.

If you lose two, it's on top of you,
    If you stand fast. And that
Could weigh on your mind until you find
    You feel like nothing in nothing flat.

Frizzing

It snew all night. By the next noon
Eleven feet of sney had snoon.
I jumped up out of bed and snoze.
The snuz stopped in midair and froze.
"Dear wife," I said, "how cold it is!"
My words fell from my lips and friz.
I shivered a whole shrig of shovers.
Said she from underneath the covers,
"Don't you know yet what time it is?
I think you should not have ariz."
And I, agreeing with her views,
Snugged back and snoze another snooze.

At the Beach

— Johnny, Johnny, let go of that crab!
   You have only ten fingers, you know:
   If you hold it that way, it is certain to grab
   At least one or two of them. Please, let go!

— Thank you, Daddy, for teaching not scolding,
   But there's one thing I think you should know:
   I believe it's the crab that is doing the holding —
   I let go — OUCH! — ten minutes ago!

It Really Wasn't Too Bad

On Monday my mother went for a ride.
    She didn't come home for a week.
She brought back a bundle. The bundle cried.
    I decided to take a peek.

It was full of a little old wrinkled thing.
    "Say hello to your brother," she said.
It looked at me and began to sing
    In a voice like a squeaky bed.

It sang for a day. It sang for a week.
    "If we have to keep it," said I,
"Let me get the oil can and fix that squeak.
    At least let me give it a try."

She gave me a bottle. "Try this instead."
      So I fed it and watched it slurp
And gurgle and gulp. And when it was fed,
      It smiled, and it gave me a burp!

"Well, now," said Mother, "that could have
   been worse."
      "Did it cost very much?" said I.
"Oh, no — a bargain. The doctor and nurse
      Both called it a very good buy."

"Let's keep it," I said, "at least for a while."
      "If you think so," said she, "I'll ask Dad."
And it heard us and started to gurgle and smile.
      And really, it wasn't too bad!

A Lesson in Manners

Someone told me someone said
You should never be bad till you've been fed.
You may, you know, be sent to bed
Without your supper. — And there you are
With nothing to eat. Not even a jar
Of pickle juice, nor a candy bar.
No, nothing to eat and nothing to drink,
And all night long to lie there and think
About washing baby's ears with ink,
Or nailing the door shut, or sassing Dad,
Or about whatever you did that was bad,
And wishing you hadn't, and feeling sad.

Now then, if what I'm told is true,
What I want to say to you — and you —
Is: MIND YOUR MANNERS. They just
   won't do.
If you have to be bad, you must learn to wait
Till after supper. Be good until eight.
If you let your badness come out late
It doesn't hurt to be sent to bed.
Well, not so much. So use your head:
Don't be bad till you've been fed.

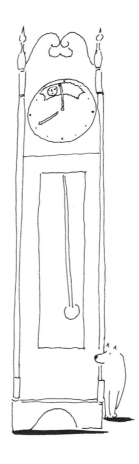

About Being Very Good and Far Better Than Most But Still Not Quite Good Enough to Take on the Atlantic Ocean

There was a fine swimmer named Jack
Who swam ten miles out — and nine back!

(What more can I tell you? That boy had style,
But in the end, he missed — by a mile.)

The Glass Canoe

There was a man in a glass canoe.
    (So he could see the fish.)
He paddled out to watch a trout.
    It gave its tail a swish.

It swished downriver. Trout can do
    A remarkable lot of swishing
When they see you in a glass canoe
    And guess you may be fishing.

It swished downriver — toward the falls,
    A rather daft thing to do.
It was even dafter to follow after,
    I'd say, in a glass canoe.

But that's what they did, and what came next
    The trout just will not say.
(I know a pool where it goes to school
    And I spoke to it there today.)

I haven't seen the glass canoe.
    I hear it tried to split
A rock in two (which it couldn't do)
    And that the rock split it.

I did see a very wet sort of man
  Come shivering out of the mist,
And I heard him sigh as he passed by,
  "I knew, but I couldn't resist!"

Then he shivered into the mist again.
  And I couldn't be sure, but I guessed
I had seen him before. If you want to know more,
  You'll have to make up the rest.

There Was a Man from Nowhere

There was a man from nowhere.
    He never got where he went.
He bought a ticket out of there.
    It cost him what he spent.

He traveled seven miles before
    He found he was on his way.
When he got back he was there once more.
    But then he couldn't stay.

He never managed to begin
    Before it was too late.
He lost all that he could not win.
    He arrived too late to wait.

His mother was his father's wife.
    He was their only son
For all the first years of his life,
    And then he was the other one.

He got these facts from a looking glass
    While standing on his head
With his eyes shut tight against the light.
    "When I do that," he said,

"I turn things shortside outside long
　　And upside downside in.
And when they say I get things wrong,
　　I grin a secret grin,

"And I look again with my eyes tight shut
　　And I never manage to see
A single thing I am wrong about.
　　— Which is good enough for me."

The Old Salt

There was a man who went to sea.
    He didn't have a ship.
"Once I have learned to swim," said he,
    "I'll take a longer trip."

He waded two feet out and there
    A wave got in his shoes.
He kicked it out and said, "Take care:
    You are spoiling my whole cruise!"

Another wave got in his eyes.
    He blinked it out and said,
"I half suspect this isn't wise.
    I'm going home to bed."

His bed was warm, his bed was dry.
    He sat on it and wrote:
"The sea is much too wet to try
    Until I have a boat."

His bed was dry, his bed was warm.
    He slept in it and made it warmer.
That night he dreamed he heard a storm
    Beating against his dormer.

He dreamed he sailed to Mandalay
    As captain of a sailing ship.
He woke and thought, "Now *there's* the way
    To take an ocean trip:

"No ship to buy, no shoes to wet.
    No seasick pills to swallow.
I like to dream of a life at sea:
    It beats all others hollow!"

Now About Tigers

Now about tigers. Notice, please,
How few of them you meet.
I've looked behind a hundred trees
On both sides of the street

And not one tiger did I see.
There *was* a tabby cat
In Willy's chinaberry tree,
But I'm not counting *that*.

Still, more or less, it looked a lot
As if it *might* have been
Almost a tiger. I half thought
That's what it was. I mean

I nearly did. But notice, please,
I changed my mind. And why? Because
I studied hard to earn straight D's
In logic and the various laws

Of everything there is to know
Before you look at what you see.
And thus I saw it wasn't so,
But just a tabby in a tree.

Unless you learn to train your mind
And study hard to earn a star
For tidy homework, you may find
More tigers than there really are.

Sometimes There Is No Easy Answer

I came to a forest so deep and wide
    And close together trees couldn't grow.
Even the birds were locked inside.
    How they got in, I'll never know.

I heard them squawk, "This is absurd!"
    — I think that's what they meant, but yes,
All I could see was what I heard,
    And some of that I had to guess.

Or guess for yourself. It breaks no law
    To be as wrong as you're sure to be.
I wasn't sure I heard what I saw,
    And it's hard to hear what you guess you see.

I'll tell you this, and it couldn't be truer:
    A forest too thick for trees to grow
Leaves room for doubt. So I can't be sure,
    But what I think is I don't know.

Good-bye

Seven cats and seven mice
Sat seven days on a cake of ice.

The trouble with sitting on ice is: it melts
And you have to go sit on something else.

The trouble with sitting beside a cat,
If you're a mouse, is: it grows fat

While you grow fewer...fewer...none!
The trouble with telling you more is: I'm done.